Why We Need a SAVIOR?

Why Do We Need a SAVIOR?

"Good People," "Bad People,"
and God's Perspective

Tracy M. Sumner

BARBOUR
PUBLISHING

Print ISBN 978-1-62416-996-0

eBook Editions:
Adobe Digital Edition (.epub) 978-1-63058-049-0
Kindle and MobiPocket Edition (.prc) 978-1-63058-050-6

Published by Barbour Publishing, Inc., P.O. Box 719, Uhrichsville, Ohio 44683, www.barbourbooks.com

Our mission is to publish and distribute inspirational products offering exceptional value and biblical encouragement to the masses.

Printed in the United States of America.

CONTENTS

Introduction 7

1. Sin: Humankind's Universal Problem . . . 13

2. How Good Is Good Enough? 45

3. Why We Need Jesus 68

4. What Must I Do. . . ? 101

5. Some FAQs about Our Need for
   the Savior 128

Conclusion 155

INTRODUCTION

Here's a scenario none of us would want to face:

A man on a long car trip is driving a remote stretch of highway in some really cold, rainy weather when his engine begins to sputter. Then, suddenly, it freezes.

The next day—after sitting for hours in his disabled vehicle, then getting a huge bill for towing—the man learns that his engine had overheated so badly it will cost thousands of dollars to repair.

What had happened? The car's thermostat had failed, leaving the engine's cooling system unable to do the work for which it was designed. Even worse, the mechanic informed the man that the car had been due for a thermostat change for some time.

The failure to replace a part costing $15 and an hour's labor ended up costing the man thousands of dollars and loads of frustration. He just didn't know he needed to replace the thermostat.

Sometimes *forewarned* truly is to be *forearmed*.

Tragically, as it pertains to spiritual life, many people are like this unfortunate motorist. In their approach to eternal destinations, they never get around to receiving the gift of forgiveness and salvation God so freely offers through Jesus Christ—because they just don't realize they need it. If they think about such things at all, many of these people go through life being "good"—in human terms—and believe they are "okay with God." They haven't committed any of the "big" sins, so they can't imagine why they shouldn't go to heaven when they die.

The biblical truth is that *everyone* needs a savior.

But missing the truth about our need for a savior is far more disastrous than even the biggest bill from a mechanic.

The biblical truth is that *everyone* needs a savior—even those who live moral, ethical lives, those who treat others with kindness and compassion, and those whose life purpose is to give of themselves to others.

Regarding our need for a savior, the Bible teaches that:

- All humans since Adam and Eve sin by what they do and what they don't do, and that sin separates them from a holy God.

- We all deserve eternal punishment for our sin.

- There is nothing any of us can do on our own to escape God's judgment and earn a place in His eternal kingdom.

- In His loving compassion for people, and because He knew we needed a Savior, God has provided a door to His kingdom of heaven, in the person of Jesus Christ, who came to earth to live a sinless life, then die a sacrificial death for the sins of all humankind.

- God's offer of salvation is open to *all* people, no matter how badly they've messed up.

- We can access God's offer of salvation only through faith in Jesus Christ.

This book is about these fundamental biblical truths. It's not just about our need for a savior, but our need for *the* Savior, Jesus Christ.

You may be a "seeker" (a person who has wondered why you need the Savior and wants to know more) or a believer who'd like to more effectively explain to your friends and family members why they need the Savior. Either way, this book can help you to better understand God's plan for salvation and why He made that plan in the first place.

Every single one of us needs the Savior,

Jesus Christ. Only He has the power and authority to save people from their sin and grant them a place in heaven. Our hope is that this book will help you to fully understand the biblical truths of God's amazing love for humankind as a whole, and for you individually.

1
SIN: HUMANKIND'S
UNIVERSAL PROBLEM

In a powerful scene in the Academy Award-winning 1992 western *Unforgiven*, an aspiring bounty hunter who calls himself the Schofield Kid is tormented with remorse after shooting a man to death as he sat virtually helpless in an outhouse. Despite his earlier arrogant claims of having killed several men, it was the first time the Kid had ever actually taken a human life.

In tears—and while making short work of a bottle of whiskey in an attempt to ease his feelings of guilt—the Kid says to his partner, William Munny, a "reformed" gunslinger played by Clint Eastwood, "It don't seem real. . .how he ain't gonna never breathe again. . .ever. . .how he's dead—and the other one, too. All on account of pulling a trigger."

Munny, who was described in the movie's prologue as "a known thief and murderer, a man of notoriously vicious and intemperate disposition," knows about these things all too well. He tells the Kid, "It's a hell of a thing, killing a man. Take away all he's got and all he's ever gonna have."

"We all have it coming, kid."

Finding no comfort in Munny's observations, the young man attempts to assuage his own guilt, saying, "Yeah, well, I guess they had it coming."

Without so much as looking back at the Kid, Munny intones, "We all have it coming, kid."

In the context of 1880s frontier justice, it could be argued that the men Munny and the Schofield Kid had just killed "had it coming." They had committed a terrible sin for which they hadn't paid a price, and those they had wronged believed they were going to get away with what they had done.

Enter Munny and the Schofield Kid, two hired killers.

There's a grain—*okay, make that a large boulder*—of biblical truth in William Munny's observation that "We all have it coming."

This may come as a shock to many people, but the Bible teaches that God has one standard for entrance into eternal heaven and for our avoidance of eternal punishment, and it's sinless perfection. No one who has sin of any kind in his record here on earth can expect to enter into God's eternal kingdom.

In the context of eternal punishment for sin, it can be said that we all have it coming.

That is the one reason we all need a Savior.

ALL HAVE SINNED...
The Bible has a lot to say about sin, which can be simply defined as falling short of

God's perfect standard in what we think, what we say, and what we do, as well as what we *fail* to think, say, and do.

The apostle John, one of Jesus' twelve original apostles and the writer of the Gospel of John, the three epistles (or letters) bearing his name, and the book of Revelation, wrote that "Everyone who sins is breaking God's law, for all sin is contrary to the law of God" (1 John 3:4 NLT). Later in 1 John, we read, "All wrongdoing is sin" (5:17 NIV).

John wanted his readers to understand that when they did the things they knew were wrong in God's eyes—or when they failed to do the things they knew He wanted them to do—they were sinning and failing to meet the standard God has set in His written Word, the Bible.

When reading the above verses, it might be tempting to think, *Well, I always try to do the right thing, always treat people correctly, and never commit any of the "big" sins like murder or adultery. I must be doing all right in God's eyes.*

Nowhere in the Bible can we find anything discouraging people from trying their best to do what is right. On the other hand—and this is vitally important to understand why we need a Savior—nowhere in the Bible can we find anything suggesting that anyone is innocent of sin.

The Bible teaches very clearly and very consistently that every human being who has ever lived or ever will live—with the exception of Jesus Christ—is a sinner who has in some way (or, in almost all cases, in *many* ways) fallen short of God's perfect standard of righteousness.

> Sin is a universal human problem.

Both the Old Testament and the New Testament tell us that sin is a universal human problem and that every human being is in need of God's forgiveness and restoration. Without that forgiveness and restoration, all people—even those whom we would consider "good people"—will one day enter into an eternity of separation from God, an eternity of punishment for the sins they have committed.

Here are some of the passages that clearly teach the universality of human sinfulness:

- "For everyone has sinned; we all fall short of God's glorious standard" (Romans 3:23 NLT).

- "Indeed, there is no one on earth who is righteous, no one who does what is right and never sins" (Ecclesiastes 7:20 NIV).

- "God looks down from heaven on all mankind to see if there are any who understand, any who seek God. Everyone has turned away, all have become corrupt; there is no one who does good, not even one" (Psalm 53:2–3 NIV).

- "All of us, like sheep, have strayed away. We have left God's paths to follow our own" (Isaiah 53:6 NLT).

- "All of us have become like one who is unclean, and all our righteous acts are like filthy rags; we all shrivel up like a leaf, and like the wind our sins sweep us away" (Isaiah 64:6 NIV).

- "What shall we conclude then? Do we have any advantage? Not at all! For we have already made the charge that Jews and Gentiles alike are all under the power of sin" (Romans 3:9 NIV).

- "If we claim to be without sin, we deceive ourselves and the truth is not in us" (1 John 1:8 NIV).

- "All have turned away; all have become corrupt. No one does good, not a single one!" (Psalm 14:3 NLT).

...Or Have They?

While the Bible contains many passages pointing to the sinfulness of all human-kind, it also includes a few accounts of people it called *blameless*, *upright*, *righteous*, and even *perfect*. Consider the following examples:

- God said of Noah, who went to incredible lengths to obey God, even though His instructions probably made little earthly sense, "I have found you righteous in this generation" (Genesis 7:1 NIV).

- Job, a model citizen and father whose story of incredible suffering is told in the Old Testament book that bears his name, was "perfect and upright, and one that feared God, and eschewed evil" (Job 1:1 KJV).

- Zacharias, first-century priest, father to John the Baptist, and husband to Elizabeth, was said to be "righteous in the sight of God, observing all the Lord's commands and decrees blamelessly" (Luke 1:6 NIV).

Some skeptics have pointed to the above passages as proof that the Bible has contradicted itself on the issue of the universality of sin in humans. At a glance, these verses appear problematic to those who hold to the biblical truth that no one is without sin in God's eyes.

But when you take a closer look at the biblical stories of these three men, you'll see that none of them was "perfect," "blameless," or "righteous" in the sense that they never sinned. In fact, the Bible specifically gives accounts of their sins.

- Noah sinned against God when he drank so much wine that he became drunk and passed out in this tent, which led to disastrous consequences for his family (see Genesis 9:18–10:32).

- Though early in his story, Job avoided the sin of charging God foolishly (see Job 1:22), the great man later admitted he had spoken ignorantly of God and said, "I abhor myself, and repent in dust and ashes" (Job 42:6 KJV).

- Zacharias sinned when he voiced doubt at the promise of God that he and his wife would have a son (John the Baptist). As a result, he was struck mute until the promise was fulfilled (see Luke 1:11–21).

The Bible teaches very clearly that only one man who ever lived was completely sinless in every way: Jesus Christ (see 2 Corinthians 5:21; 1 Peter 2:22; Hebrews 4:15, 7:26, 9:14; 1 John 3:5). So when it refers to certain people as "righteous" or "blameless," it isn't saying that they never struggled with sin the same way all people do, only that they loved God and were committed to keeping His commandments.

The apostle James hinted at the sinfulness of humans, even when they outwardly obey the laws of God: "If you really keep the royal law found in Scripture, 'Love your neighbor as yourself,' you are doing right. But if you show favoritism, you sin and are convicted by the law as lawbreakers. For whoever keeps the whole law and yet stumbles at just one point is guilty of breaking all of it" (James 2:8–10 NIV).

Simply put, in an eternal sense, this verse means that if you have committed one "small" sin, such as telling a "white lie" or thinking an impure thought about your attractive coworker, then you are just as guilty before

> God has set one standard for all people, and it is sinless perfection.

God as if you've committed murder or adultery.

That sounds harsh to the human mind, but it points to how seriously God takes *all* sin. God has set one standard for all people, and it is sinless perfection. God does not "grade on a curve." He set His standards in eternity past, and He will keep those standards for eternity future. His standards have nothing to do with human merit or with anyone's standing or reputation among other people. And when we mess up in even what we might consider the smallest areas, we are guilty in God's eyes of messing up in every area.

The apostle Paul, writing to Christians in an ancient city called Corinth, listed "wrongdoers" who would not see the kingdom of heaven because of their sin: "Do you not know that wrongdoers will not inherit the kingdom of God? Do not be deceived: Neither the sexually immoral nor idolaters nor adulterers nor men who have sex with men nor thieves nor the greedy nor drunkards nor slanderers nor swindlers will inherit the kingdom of God" (1 Corinthians 6:9–10 NIV).

The sins listed in that passage look like "biggies," don't they? But in another passage, Paul repeated his warning, adding other sins, some of which don't seem quite as serious, that would keep people out of heaven: "When you follow the desires of your sinful nature, the results are very clear: sexual immorality, impurity, lustful pleasures, idolatry, sorcery, hostility, quarreling, jealousy, outbursts of anger, selfish ambition, dissension, division, envy, drunkenness, wild parties, and other sins like these. Let me tell you again, as I have before, that anyone living that sort of life will not inherit the Kingdom of God" (Galatians 5:19–21 NLT).

That's pretty dire news for all of humanity, isn't it? Every human but one has sinned in some way (most of us in one or more of the ways Paul listed above, and many in ways he didn't include on his lists), and that sin will bar us from being reconciled with God and welcomed into His eternal home in heaven. Furthermore, that sin we have all committed sentences us to

> Sin will bar us from being reconciled with God and welcomed into His eternal home in heaven.

eternal punishment in a terrible place called hell.

The Bible not only teaches us that all human beings born since Adam and Eve are sinners—people whose natures, actions, words, and thoughts are imperfect—it also uses some very direct language to describe sinners. Here are some examples:

- Children of disobedience (Ephesians 2:2)

- Children of hell (Matthew 23:15)

- Children of the bondwoman (Galatians 4:31)

- Children of the devil (1 John 3:10)

- Children of the wicked one (Matthew 13:38)

- Children of this world (Luke 16:8)

- Children of wrath (Ephesians 2:3)

- Cursed children (2 Peter 2:14)

- Enemies of the cross (Philippians 3:18)

- Enemies of righteousness (Acts 13:10)

- Evildoers (Psalm 37:9)

- Fools (Psalm 53:1)

- Reprobates (2 Corinthians 13:5)

- Transgressors (Psalm 37:38)

- Vessels of wrath (Romans 9:22)

In the biblical sense, we can look at the prospect of eternal separation from God and eternal punishment and say with all honesty, "We all have it coming." All of us have sinned—in fact, some of us have made certain types of sin a chosen lifestyle—and that means we have no hope, apart from an act on the part of God Himself, of escaping eternal punishment.

> God has made a way to be reconciled with Him.

But here is the good news: God has made a way to be reconciled with Him and to spend eternity in heaven. We will get to that in more depth later, but for now, let's take a closer look at why all humans—every man, woman, and child—so desperately need a Savior.

WHERE IT ALL STARTED: THE PROBLEM OF ORIGINAL SIN

The Bible teaches that every human being who is a descendant of Adam and Eve—and that would be *all* people—is born with a sinful nature, and that this nature will lead them to commit sins against God and against one another. This is what Bible scholars and theologians call "original sin."

You won't find the actual term "original sin"—which is also sometimes called "inherited sin"—anywhere in the Bible. But several Bible passages strongly point to the truth that each of us is under a curse of sin because of Adam and Eve's sin:

- "Behold, I was brought forth in iniquity, and in sin my mother conceived me" (Psalm 51:5 NKJV).

- "When Adam sinned, sin entered the world. Adam's sin brought death, so death spread to everyone, for everyone sinned" (Romans 5:12 NLT).

- "For since death came through a man, the resurrection of the dead comes also through a man. For as in Adam all die, so in Christ all will be made alive" (1 Corinthians 15:21–22 NIV).

"Original sin" separated all humans from God.

You can find the story of how "original sin"—the result of what is often referred to as "the Fall" or "the Fall of Man"—separated all humans from God in the first three chapters of the book of Genesis.

The very first biblical proclamation of God's role as our Creator appears in Genesis 1:1, "In the beginning God created the heavens and the earth." The first chapter of Genesis gives a detailed account of God creating something perfect: the earth that would be home to humanity (1:2–9); sunlight, which would allow living things to see and which would provide the energy needed to sustain life on earth (1:3–4); the plants, which would feed all living things on earth (1:11–12); the entire cosmos, including the sun, the moon, the stars, and other celestial bodies (1:14-19); every kind of swimming and land-dwelling animal (1:20-25); and, finally, humans themselves (1:26–28).

But there was something very different about the way in which God designed humans. As He formed mankind out of dust, He said, "Let Us make man *in Our image, according to Our likeness*; let them have dominion over the fish of the sea, over the birds of the air, and over the cattle, over all the earth and over every creeping thing that creeps on the earth" (Genesis 1:26 NKJV, emphasis added).

God had created every living thing that flies, walks, crawls, or swims, but humans were the only thing He created in His own image. The phrase "in Our image" refers to several traits all people share. God made us very much like Himself in that we have the unique ability to think rationally and make decisions based on those thoughts.

We are also made in God's image in that we desire fellowship and interaction—both with fellow humans and with the God who created us. Of all the living things on earth, only humans have what can be called "God awareness," meaning we have the unique ability to know our Creator on a personal level.

God originally created humans to live in an eternal state of perfection. He intended for Adam and Eve, as well as their offspring, to live eternally and in complete dependence on their Creator and in complete harmony with one another. But, being the loving Creator He is, God also created them

> God originally created humans to live in an eternal state of perfection.

with a free will, meaning they could choose whether or not to enjoy unbroken fellowship with Him and whether or not to live in complete obedience to His commands.

God placed the first two humans in a perfect paradise called the Garden of Eden. They were free to do whatever they wanted, eat whatever they wanted, and to begin populating the earth with more humans. And they could enjoy perfect fellowship with their Creator.

Under one condition.

God warned Adam that he was not to

eat from the tree of knowledge of good and evil, and that doing so would result in death: "From any tree of the garden you may eat freely; but from the tree of the knowledge of good and evil you shall not eat, for in the day that you eat from it you will surely die" (Genesis 2:16–17 NASB).

As long as Adam and Eve stayed away from the "forbidden fruit," things were perfect for them. They fellowshipped with one another and with God, and there was no guilt or shame, even though they walked around the garden completely naked (see Genesis 2:25).

But everything changed forever one day when a snake—actually the devil in the body of a serpent—approached Eve and began twisting what God had said about eating from the tree of the knowledge of good and evil.

The devil is a crafty snake, and he attacked Eve at a point where he knew he could find weakness. He started by subtly twisting what God had actually said, asking her, "Did God really say, 'You must not eat from any tree in the garden'?" (Genesis 3:1 NIV).

At first, Eve had a perfect answer for the devil's deception: "We may eat fruit from the trees in the garden, but God did say, 'You must not eat fruit from the tree that is in the middle of the garden, and you must not touch it, or you will die'" (3:2–3 NIV).

But the devil wasn't about to give up. Instead, he began attacking Eve at a point where he continues to tempt people today—the desire to be independent from God and to be our own "god."

> The devil continues to tempt people today.

"'You will not certainly die,' the serpent said to the woman. 'For God knows that when you eat from it your eyes will be opened, and you will be like God, knowing good and evil'" (3:4–5 NIV).

Tragically, Eve believed the snake's lie that she wouldn't really die if she ate from the forbidden tree. She took fruit from the tree God had commanded her and her husband not to eat from, ate it, and then gave some of the fruit to Adam. That one act of disobedience threw what had been a perfect creation into chaos, where it has remained to this day.

THE CONSEQUENCES OF SIN

As much as many people don't like hearing it, sin has consequences—both in this life and in the next. All throughout the Bible, we see examples of how sin has cost the human race, starting with the first two humans.

> Sin has consequences.

When Adam and Eve chose to question God's commands, when they chose to doubt that His one prohibition in the Garden of Eden was for His glory and for their very best, they chose disobedience. The consequences of their choice were disastrous.

- Where before they stood before God naked and unashamed, they now felt guilt, shame, and embarrassment (Genesis 3:7–8)

- Eve would experience "multiplied pain" in childbirth (Genesis 3:16)

- There would be marital strife between Adam and Eve (Genesis 3:16)

- The soil would be cursed, resulting in worthless "thorns and thistles" (Genesis 3:17–18)

- They would have to struggle to make a living from the earth (Genesis 3:19)

- They would one day experience physical death (Genesis 2:16–17, 3:19)

- They lost their innocence (Genesis 3:22)

- They were forbidden from eating of the "tree of life," which represented eternal life (Genesis 3:22)

- They were banished from Eden, which was a picture of perfect fellowship with God (Genesis 3:23)

And, of course, there was death. God had given Adam and Eve complete run of the Garden of Eden and told them they could eat the fruit of any tree there except one. He also warned Adam that if he failed in obeying that one limitation, "you will surely die" (Genesis 2:17).

And die they most certainly did.

Adam and Eve didn't physically die immediately after they chose to disobey God. The Bible tells us that Adam lived for 930 years (see Genesis 5:5) and that he and his wife had at least seven children, three of whom are named in the Bible: Cain, Abel, and Seth. However, their once-perfect bodies did eventually wear down, and they ultimately died physically. But the worst death—a spiritual one—they suffered almost immediately as they were banished from the Garden and from perfect communion with God.

> Adam and Eve were banished from the Garden and from perfect communion with God.

Tragically, the spiritual death Adam and Eve suffered that day wasn't limited to just these two disobedient people. Sin and its resulting spiritual death—and eventual physical death for all of humanity—spread like a contagion from Adam and Eve to every human born after them. As a result of this one act of disobedience, everyone who is a descendant of Adam and Eve, meaning every human being who has lived or ever will live, is born into a fallen, sinful world and possesses a fallen, sinful nature.

OUR DIAGNOSIS: "DEAD IN SIN"

Thousands of years after Adam and Eve chose disobedience over perfect fellowship with God, the apostle Paul wrote, "The wages of sin is death" (Romans 6:23). The biblical truth is that because of Adam and Eve's disobedience, we are all sinners, and as sinners, we die spiritually because our sin separates us from God, who is our source of life.

You don't need a license to practice medicine—or even an especially extensive knowledge of how the human body works—to know that the absolute worst diagnosis a patient can receive is "dead." When someone is pronounced "dead on arrival," there is nothing even the best medical talent in the world can do to change it. "Dead" truly means dead!

The Bible gives that same chilling diagnosis to those who don't know Jesus Christ as their Savior. Writing to the first-century church in a city called Ephesus, Paul pointed out to these Christians that they had once been "dead in [their] transgressions and sins in which [they] used to live when [they] followed in the ways of this world and of the ruler of the kingdom of the air, the spirit who is now at work in those who are disobedient" (Ephesians 2:1–2 NIV; also see Ephesians 2:5; Colossians 2:13).

This death is the curse Adam wrought on the entire human race when he chose to disobey God back in the Garden of Eden, and it's a curse on each and every one of us because of our own sinful nature and our own sinful thoughts, words, and actions.

> Death is the curse Adam wrought on the entire human race.

Obviously, the term "dead in sin" does not refer to physical death—even though that is one of the consequences of sin. Today, sinful people—people whose actions, words, and thoughts demonstrate that they don't know God—can live very long and healthy physical lives and are more than able to make decisions based on their own wills.

So if sinful people are apparently alive in every way we can observe, what does "dead in sin" mean? Paul was referring to spiritual death, which is the condition of every human who is separated from God due to sin.

The person who is dead in sin is completely unable to trust or believe God or to live a life that pleases God. Paul, writing to another church—this one in ancient Rome—said, "For the sinful nature is always hostile to God. It never did obey God's laws, and it never will. That's why those who are still under the control of their sinful nature can never please God" (Romans 8:7–8 NLT).

Paul went even further in his description of those who need a Savior when he wrote to the ancient church in Corinth, "The person without the Spirit does not accept the things that come from the Spirit of God but considers them foolishness, and cannot understand them because they are discerned only through the Spirit" (1 Corinthians 2:14 NIV).

We are all spiritually dead because of our individual chosen sin, and we are spiritually dead because of the sin nature we inherited from Adam and Eve. Because of that, we are incapable of doing anything to please God or to earn His forgiveness for our sin.

Yes, we have a huge problem, one that keeps us from God and will result in our eternal separation from Him. God has set a standard of thinking, speaking, and behavior that *no one* can keep perfectly, and that means that even those we consider the very best the human race has to offer are guilty before Him.

> We are incapable of doing anything to please God or to earn His forgiveness.

Jesus told His twelve apostles—the men He had chosen to spread the Good News of salvation throughout the world after He returned to heaven—"Apart from me, you can do nothing" (John 15:5 NIV). Earlier, He told them that people can't even come to God "unless the Father who sent me draws them" (John 6:44 NIV).

We are truly incapable of doing anything

apart from Christ, simply because we are spiritually dead. The word picture of "dead in sin" is especially apt because the Bible teaches that there is nothing we can do, apart from Christ, to earn God's favor or forgiveness.

But the Bible promises us that an eternally loving God has done for us what we can't do on our own: "But because of his great love for us, God, who is rich in mercy, made us alive with Christ even when we were dead in transgressions—it is by grace you have been saved" (Ephesians 2:4–5 NIV).

Furthermore, God did for us what we couldn't do for ourselves before we even knew we needed it: "But God demonstrates his own love for us in this: While we were still sinners, Christ died for us" (Romans 5:8 NIV).

Eternal separation from God and eternal punishment for our sins— they're something we all have coming to us. We're all hopelessly lost and dead in our sins against God. But in the greatest act of love in all eternity,

> God provided for us what we could never provide for ourselves.

a passionately loving God who knew just how much we needed a Savior provided for us what we could never provide for ourselves.

2
HOW GOOD IS
GOOD ENOUGH?

In the last chapter, you read that every human being ever born—with the exception of Jesus Christ—has sinned, sometimes in terrible ways. You also read that while we as humans can be tempted into thinking that God will overlook "small" sins and that He only punishes really evil people, the scriptural truth is that God sees all sin the same and that He must punish all sin.

Since sin separates humanity from God, then all humans need forgiveness and salvation if we want to spend eternity in heaven. But the question so many ask is, "How good of a person do I need to be to get into heaven and avoid eternal punishment in hell?"

Many people—particularly those who don't know the Bible very well—ascribe to a "balance sheet" way of looking at their own sin. They believe that if they do more good things than bad things, they'll make it to heaven. Others believe that if they spend their lives "making up for" some evil thing they did years ago, then God won't hold their sins against them. After all, as long as the balance sheet shows that our good deeds outweigh our bad deeds (our sins), God will certainly let us into heaven —won't He?

But that isn't what the Bible teaches. On the contrary, the Bible teaches that a person's eternal salvation has nothing to do with his or her own "goodness" but everything to do with the goodness and mercy God demonstrated in sending the Savior.

Put simply, doing bad things and being a "bad person" (sinning) will keep you

> Doing good things and being a "good person" won't get you into heaven.

46

out of heaven, but doing good things and being a "good person" won't get you into heaven.

GOD'S WRITTEN STANDARDS FOR "GOODNESS"

Most religious belief systems (or systems that hold to the belief in a personal deity) have their own codes of ethics and instructions for how to live in a way that pleases their own particular god. Judaism, which God in His own timing used to bring the Savior, Jesus Christ, into the world, has one of its own.

In the first five books of the Hebrew Bible (what Christians call the "Old Testament"), you can read what both the Old and New Testaments call "the Law"—or the "Law of Moses." The Law of Moses contains hundreds of rules and guidelines for living a moral life and worshiping God, as well as observing civil and dietary practices.

Writers of the Old and New Testament scripture had nothing but good things to say about God's Law. Here are just a few of many examples:

- "I desire to do your will, my God; your law is within my heart" (Psalm 40:8 NIV).

- "Open my eyes, that I may see wondrous things from Your law" (Psalm 119:18 NKJV).

- "Oh, how I love your law! I meditate on it all day long" (Psalm 119:97 NIV).

- "It pleased the LORD for the sake of his righteousness to make his law great and glorious" (Isaiah 42:21 NIV).

- "So then, the law is holy, and the commandment is holy, righteous and good" (Romans 7:12 NIV).

- "For in my inner being I delight in God's law" (Romans 7:22 NIV).

Obviously, the people who recorded the words we have in our Bible today held the Law of God in very high esteem. They memorized it, studied it, quoted it, and, as best they could, they lived by it.

But as important as the Law is, the Bible teaches that God has imposed limitations on it. For one thing, as hard as people may try, no one can keep the Law perfectly—which is God's one standard for righteousness.

> As hard as people may try, no one can keep the Law perfectly.

The apostle Paul clarified for Christians the role God intended for the Law in bringing salvation to the whole world when he wrote, "Obviously, the law applies to those to whom it was given, for its purpose is to keep people from having excuses, and to show that the entire world is guilty before God. For no one can ever be made right with God by doing what the law commands. The law simply shows us how sinful we are" (Romans 3:19–20 NLT).

This means that the Old Testament Law, while it was given as a standard of behavior for those living in the Hebrew nation of Israel, was also intended as a standard by which all humans can measure their own "goodness" as well as what is sin and what isn't. Without the Law, we would have no way of knowing what God expects of us—or what to do when we fail to live up to His standards.

And, as the Bible so clearly teaches, all humans fail to keep the Law perfectly.

SAVED BY KEEPING GOD'S LAW?

When you read what the New Testament has to say about why we need a Savior, it's important to understand that most of these books were written by Jewish people who had some understanding of the Law of God as it was handed down during Old

Testament times. (The exceptions would be the Gospel of Luke and the book of Acts, which were written by a Gentile named Luke.)

The New Testament books were also written at a time when many Christians—especially Jewish converts—had some serious questions about what keeping the Law had to do with their personal salvation.

In chapter 1 of this book, you read how the Bible leaves no doubt that every human being who lives, has ever lived, or ever will live is a sinner in need of God's mercy and forgiveness. You read how every one of us, because we are imperfect humans with natures that are prone to sin, has failed in some way (most of us in many ways) of living up to God's standards of sinless perfection.

> Every one of us, has failed in some way.

As an expert on the Law who also happened to be a sinful human being (see Romans 7:14–20), the apostle Paul knew as well as anyone that no human was capable of keeping it perfectly. But as a man who understood the ultimate purpose of the Law, he repeatedly wrote that it was faith in Jesus Christ the Savior, not obedience to the Law, that saved people.

- "For this reason it is by faith, in order that it may be in accordance with grace, so that the promise will be guaranteed to all the descendants, not only to those who are of the Law, but also to those who are of the faith of Abraham, who is the father of us all" (Romans 4:16 NASB).

- "Christ is the culmination of the law so that there may be righteousness for everyone who believes" (Romans 10:4 NIV).

- "Yet we know that a person is made right with God by faith in Jesus Christ, not by obeying the law. And we have believed in Christ Jesus, so that we might be made right with God because of our faith in Christ, not because we have obeyed the law. For no one will ever be made right with God by obeying the law" (Galatians 2:16 NLT).

- "I do not set aside the grace of God, for if righteousness could be gained through the law, Christ died for nothing!" (Galatians 2:21 NIV).

- "So again I ask, does God give you his Spirit and work miracles among you by the works of the law, or by your believing what you heard? So also Abraham 'believed God, and it was credited to him as righteousness'" (Galatians 3:5–6 NIV).

- "So the law was our guardian until Christ came that we might be justified by faith. Now that this faith has come, we are no longer under a guardian" (Galatians 3:24–25 NIV).

- "...be found in Him, not having my own righteousness, which is from the law, but that which is through faith in Christ, the righteousness which is from God by faith" (Philippians 3:9 NKJV).

But what about these words, also from the pen of the scholar Paul: "When the Gentiles sin, they will be destroyed, even though they never had God's written law. And the Jews, who do have God's law, will be judged by that law when they fail to obey it. For merely listening to the law doesn't make us right with God. It is obeying the law that makes us right in his sight" (Romans 2:12–13 NLT).

Taken by itself, this passage seems to be telling us that without obedience to Old Testament Law, none of us can be saved. Is this a contradiction? A misprint? Or is there something else important at work here?

Taken in the context of the rest of the Bible on this subject, it is apparent that

Paul is simply pointing out that people who believed they could be saved by keeping the Law could only "earn" eternal life by keeping every single detail of that Law perfectly. If they kept every single Law except one, then they were in trouble because only those who were perfect "doers" of the Law could be justified.

It was almost as if he were writing, "You want to be saved by keeping the Law? Well, have at it. But I must warn you that if you fail at any point—and I mean even the smallest little detail—then you'll be lost for eternity. And, by the way, you're going to fail, simply because no one other than Jesus has ever kept the Law perfectly. You don't have the aptitude to obey the Law perfectly. You're going to fail, and it's going to cost you everything. That is why you need a Savior! That is why you need Jesus!"

> "You're going to fail, and it's going to cost you everything. That is why you need a Savior!"

It's also why he wrote later in the book of Romans, "For we maintain that a person is justified by faith apart from the works of the law" (3:28 NIV).

THE SAVIOR:
THE FULFILLMENT OF THE LAW

Matthew 5–7 is an amazing passage of scripture that recounts Jesus' famous "Sermon on the Mount," which is made up of tough-but-practical teachings regarding the Law and life. In this sermon, Jesus clarified and enlarged on many of the Old Testament laws, adding a "spirit-of-the-law" twist many of His followers had never before heard.

Speaking specifically of the Law and what it had to do with His mission and message, Jesus said:

> *Don't misunderstand why I have come. I did not come to abolish the law of Moses or the writings of the prophets. No, I came to accomplish their purpose. I tell*

you the truth, until heaven and earth disappear, not even the smallest detail of God's law will disappear until its purpose is achieved. So if you ignore the least commandment and teach others to do the same, you will be called the least in the Kingdom of Heaven. But anyone who obeys God's laws and teaches them will be called great in the Kingdom of Heaven.

MATTHEW 5:17–20 NLT

That phrase, "I came to accomplish their purpose," is an important one. In one sense, it means that Christ came to fulfill the entirety of the Old Testament, including the hundreds of prophecies about the coming of the Messiah. But He also came to fulfill all the Old Testament-era requirements regarding sacrifices people had to make to atone for

> When Jesus died on the cross, it was a once-and-for-all sacrifice for the sins of all humans.

sin (see Leviticus 4:35, 5:10). When Jesus died on the cross, it was a once-and-for-all sacrifice for the sins of all humans (see Hebrews 10:1–18).

Contrary to what many of His enemies (the religious teachers of His day) claimed, Jesus didn't oppose the Law. He loved the Law, and was the only one ever to obey it perfectly. What He did was remove the curse from people for failing to adhere to it perfectly and establish a new system in which people related to God by faith (see Galatians 3:10–13). No longer was perfect obedience to the Law a requirement for entrance into heaven.

That is largely why Jesus said of a certain group of Jewish religious leaders of His day, "For I tell you that unless your righteousness surpasses that of the Pharisees and the teachers of the law, you will certainly not enter the kingdom of heaven" (Matthew 5:20 NIV).

If you know a little something about most of the Pharisees and teachers of the Law living at that time, then you understand just how strong Jesus' words about them really were. The Pharisees were experts on the Law, and they were very meticulous about keeping it, as well as the rules and regulations that had been added to it over time, to the very letter. They were so extreme in their adherence to the tiniest details of the Law that they missed the bigger picture of why God gave people the Law in the first place.

When Jesus said that people's righteousness must surpass that of the Pharisees, He was drawing attention to two things: 1. Obsessive Law-keeping didn't achieve the high standards of righteousness God requires, and 2. The spirit of the Law (truly loving God and neighbor) was more important than the letter of the Law.

WHAT ABOUT DOING GOOD— FOR GOD AND FOR OTHERS?

Ask the man or the woman in the street what will secure a person's place in God's eternal heaven, and you're likely to hear an answer along the lines of, "being a good person and doing good things for other people."

There's no question that the Bible contains many instructions concerning how Christians should behave. It commands/encourages us to treat others fairly and justly, to have compassion on those who aren't as well off as we are, and to give financially to those who do God's work—among many others. Not only that, it promises rewards in heaven for good works (see Matthew 16:27; Luke 6:23; Revelation 22:12).

But does simply doing those things out of the goodness of our own hearts guarantee us a place in God's eternal kingdom? No, it doesn't! You can't "earn" your way into heaven by doing good deeds any more than you can earn your way into heaven by strictly adhering to the letter of the Law of Moses.

> You can't "earn" your way into heaven.

Jesus pointed out that a lot of people who do a lot of good things—even in His name—wouldn't necessarily go to heaven:

Not everyone who calls out to me, "Lord! Lord!" will enter the Kingdom of Heaven. Only those who actually do the will of my Father in heaven will enter. On judgment day many will say to me, "Lord! Lord! We prophesied in your name and cast out demons in your name and performed many miracles in your name." But I will reply, "I never knew you. Get away from me, you who break God's laws."

MATTHEW 7:21–23 NLT

Christianity, while it is partially based on biblical instructions for living a life that pleases God, is different from the world's religions in that it teaches that salvation isn't *based* on what we can do for God or for others but on what God has done for us—namely providing us a Savior. In other words, while many religions are works-based, Christianity is based solely in God's work and God's unmerited favor on us.

There is nothing you can add to what

Jesus has done on the Cross. He has already done everything needed to pay for your sins and put you at peace with God—a God of grace and mercy:

- "And if by grace, then it is no longer of works; otherwise grace is no longer grace. But if it is of works, it is no longer grace; otherwise work is no longer work" (Romans 11:6 NKJV).

- "God saved you by his grace when you believed. And you can't take credit for this; it is a gift from God. Salvation is not a reward for the good things we have done, so none of us can boast about it" (Ephesians 2:8–9 NLT).

- "He saved us, not because of the righteous things we had done, but because of his mercy" (Titus 3:5 NLT).

WHO IS "GOOD ENOUGH" TO BE SAVED?

At one point in His Sermon on the Mount, Jesus spoke these troublesome, even frightening, words to His followers: "But you are to be perfect, even as your Father in heaven is perfect" Matthew 5:48 NLT).

As you read those words of the Savior, you might be thinking,

Wait a minute! I've been reading in this book that there is nothing I can do in my own power to make myself "good enough" for God. And now Jesus is saying I have to be perfect? If He's saying we are to be perfect, then who can possibly be saved?

You wouldn't be the first to ask that question. After witnessing an exchange between Jesus and a rich young man who appeared to be a good person and hearing what Jesus had to say about the conversation, the Twelve seemed genuinely

"I tell you the truth, it is very hard for a rich person to enter the Kingdom of Heaven."

disturbed at what they had just heard: "I tell you the truth, it is very hard for a rich person to enter the Kingdom of Heaven. I'll say it again—it is easier for a camel to go through the eye of a needle than for a rich person to enter the Kingdom of God!" (Matthew 19:23–24 NLT).

In Jewish culture of that time, wealth was often seen as a sign of God's blessing on a man. And not only was this young man materially blessed, he also seemed to genuinely care about his own eternal destination. He had asked Jesus what he needed to do to inherit eternal salvation, and Jesus replied that he needed to start by keeping all the commandments (vss. 18–19).

When the young man told Jesus that he had kept all the most important commandments, Jesus responded, "If you want to be perfect, go and sell all your possessions and give the money to the poor, and you will have treasure in heaven. Then come, follow me" (vs. 21).

At that, the young man, unwilling to part with his considerable worldly riches, sadly walked away from Jesus, never to be heard from again in the pages of scripture.

The disciples were astonished at what they had just witnessed. If anyone seemed like a sure-fire candidate for heaven, it was this guy. "Then who in the world can be saved?" they asked.

Jesus had the disciples right where He wanted them. It was time to give them some important teaching about how salvation works—and about what the words *good* and *perfect* really mean in the eternal context.

"Humanly speaking, it is impossible," Jesus said. "But with God everything is possible."

By this time, Jesus wasn't talking just about rich men, but about all people. He wanted His disciples to understand that, humanly speaking, it truly is impossible (not just difficult) for any person—no matter the gender, the social standing, or the works that he or she does—to be saved from eternal punishment for sin.

At the core, the answer to the question *who can be saved?* is a simple but profound one: Without God stepping in and providing our righteousness through the work of the Savior, *no one* can be saved. Obeying a set of rules won't do it, and neither will doing a bunch of good things for other people and for God. Without God doing the work, none of us can ever be good enough to be welcomed into God's eternal kingdom.

> Without God stepping in no one can be saved.

The Bible says that we are saved only through the loving provision of our Creator and not through anything we do or don't do (see Ephesians 2:8–9). That is because we are spiritually dead and incapable of pleasing God in any way.

You see, God knew from the very beginning that we all need a Savior, but not just any Savior. We need a Savior who can do for us what we could never do for ourselves, namely make us perfect in God's eyes.

And that is exactly the Savior He provided in the person of Jesus Christ.

3
WHY WE NEED JESUS

Modern culture is very democratic (if the majority of people believe something is true, then it must be true) and very individualistic (everyone has to find his or her own way) in its thinking.

Few virtues surpass that of "tolerance" in the eyes of most people. We are taught that we should be open-minded toward every belief system and every lifestyle choice, that truth is subjective, and that every human being must find his or her own way in this life.

That is especially true in areas such as religion, spirituality, and eternity. If you were to conduct a "man on the street" survey, you'd likely find a large majority of people stating their positions on eternal salvation in ways very similar to these:

- "As long as you are sincere in what you believe, then that's good enough for God."

- "We all have to find our own way."

- "There are many paths to God, and we have to find the one that works best for us."

- "God has sent a lot of messengers into the world—Moses, Jesus, Mohammed, Buddha, Confucius, and many others—and it's up to us to decide which message we want to believe."

Humanly speaking, the idea that we can all pick which path we want to take toward God sounds appealing. There are, after all, a lot of paths to choose from. But this is not what the Bible teaches. Nor is it what Jesus Himself taught.

JESUS' "INTOLERANT" MESSAGE

We've all heard people pointing to Jesus as a picture of tolerance, as someone who taught that no one has the right to judge anyone else's belief system or lifestyle choice. A good Christian—this line of thinking would suggest—is someone who follows Jesus' example by keeping his or her mouth shut when someone espouses beliefs that contradict biblical standards.

Jesus certainly had a lot to say about how those who followed Him are to treat all people—even people who don't follow Him, even people whose lifestyles and beliefs go against everything He and His Father in heaven stood for. He also practiced what He preached, spending most of His time with sinners instead of the most "religious" people of the day.

> Jesus preached a very narrow—some would say intolerant—message.

But when it came to eternity and the conditions for salvation, Jesus preached a very narrow—some would say intolerant—

message. He knew His ultimate mission, and that was to proclaim the one and only salvation message and then to give His life so that people could be reconciled to God. That is why He said, "Enter through the narrow gate. For wide is the gate and broad is the road that leads to destruction, and many enter through it. But small is the gate and narrow the road that leads to life, and only a few find it" (Matthew 7:13–14 NIV).

That was an offensive message to many people who heard Him speak it, and it remains an offensive message to many people today. Human nature being what it is, most people don't like having conditions placed on anything, including the conditions for eternal life in heaven.

But Jesus knew well God's conditions for salvation, and He courageously preached them from the start of His ministry on earth until He returned home to heaven after His death and resurrection:

- "Everyone who hears these words of Mine and does not act on them, will be like a foolish man who built his house on the sand. The rain fell, and the floods came, and the winds blew and slammed against that house; and it fell—and great was its fall" (Matthew 7:26–27 NASB).

- "Whoever acknowledges me before others, I will also acknowledge before my Father in heaven. But whoever disowns me before others, I will disown before my Father in heaven" (Matthew 10:32–33 NIV).

- "Whoever listens to you listens to me; whoever rejects you rejects me; but whoever rejects me rejects him who sent me" (Luke 10:16 NIV).

- "Also I say to you, whoever confesses Me before men, him the Son of Man also will confess before the angels of God. But he who denies Me before men will be denied before the angels of God" (Luke 12:8–9 NKJV).

- "He who believes in Him is not condemned; but he who does not believe is condemned already, because he has not believed in the name of the only begotten Son of God" (John 3:18 NKJV).

- "Whoever believes in the Son has eternal life, but whoever rejects the Son will not see life, for God's wrath remains on them" (John 3:36 NIV).

- "For the Father judges no one, but has committed all judgment to the Son, that all should honor the Son just as they honor the Father. He who does not honor the Son does not honor the Father who sent Him" (John 5:22–23 NKJV).

- "I am the light of the world. Whoever follows me will never walk in darkness, but will have the light of life" (John 8:12 NIV).

- "You are from below, I am from above; you are of this world, I am not of this world. Therefore I said to you that you will die in your sins; for unless you believe that I am He, you will die in your sins" (John 8:23–24 NASB).

- "Very truly I tell you, I am the gate for the sheep. All who have come before me are thieves and robbers, but the sheep have not listened to them" (John 10:7–8 NIV).

- "I am the way, and the truth, and the life; no one comes to the Father but through Me" (John 14:6–7 NASB).

Jesus knew very well who He was and what He had come to earth to accomplish. He knew He was the only one who could accomplish what none of us could accomplish for ourselves. Put simply, He wasn't just a man; He was also God in the flesh.

A CONSISTENT BIBLICAL MESSAGE: JESUS IS THE ONLY WAY!

Jesus repeatedly made it clear that He alone can provide humans access to God, forgiveness of sins, and eternal life in heaven. And those He chose as His apostles—the men who would communicate His message of salvation to the world around them after He returned to heaven—preached and wrote that very same message:

The apostle Peter (one of Jesus' original Twelve):

- "Jesus is 'the stone you builders rejected, which has become the cornerstone.' Salvation is found in no one else, for there is no other name under heaven given to mankind by which we must be saved" (Acts 4:11–12 NIV).

The apostle Paul and his partner-in-missions Silas:

- "And he brought them out and said, 'Sirs, what must I do to be saved?' So they said, 'Believe on the Lord Jesus Christ, and you will be saved, you and your household'" (Acts 16:30–31 NKJV).

The apostle Paul in his letters to first-century churches and church leaders:

- "If you confess with your mouth that Jesus is Lord and believe in your heart that God raised him from the dead, you will be saved. For it is by believing in your heart that you are made right with God, and it is by confessing with

your mouth that you are saved"
(Romans 10:9–10 NLT).

- "For no man can lay a foundation
  other than the one which is laid,
  which is Jesus Christ" (1 Corinthians 3:11 NASB).

- ". . .dealing out retribution to
  those who do not know God and
  to those who do not obey the gospel of our Lord Jesus" (2 Thessalonians 1:8 NASB).

- "For there is one God and one
  mediator between God and mankind, the man Christ Jesus, who
  gave himself as a ransom for all
  people" (1 Timothy 2:5–6 NIV).

- "For it is for this we labor and
  strive, because we have fixed our
  hope on the living God, who is the
  Savior of all men, especially of believers" (1 Timothy 4:10 NASB).

The apostle John (another of Jesus' original Twelve):

- "Yet to all who did receive him, to those who believed in his name, he gave the right to become children of God" (John 1:12 NIV).

- "No one who denies the Son has the Father; whoever acknowledges the Son has the Father also" (1 John 2:23 NIV).

- "And this is the testimony: God has given us eternal life, and this life is in his Son. Whoever has the Son has life; whoever does not have the Son of God does not have life" (1 John 5:11–12 NIV).

Any honest reading of the Bible will lead to the conclusion that its message of salvation is a very narrow one—as there truly is only one way to be saved, and that's through the "narrow door" of Jesus Christ.

But God didn't just *tell* us that Jesus Christ is the only way to salvation—He also *showed* us.

JESUS' QUALIFICATIONS AS SAVIOR

The biblical message of salvation through Jesus Christ alone doesn't appear in some kind of vacuum. God hasn't simply demanded that people who want to be saved engage in some kind of "blind faith" in Jesus. On the contrary, He has provided many biblical promises and proofs as to who Jesus was and to His credentials and qualifications as Savior:

1. JESUS FULFILLED ALL OLD TESTAMENT PROPHECIES ABOUT THE SAVIOR.

Not long after Adam and Eve disobeyed God and brought sin into the human condition, God made His first promise of a Messiah, or Savior, who would come into the world to provide forgiveness of sin.

Speaking to the serpent (the devil) who had deceived Adam and Eve, God said:

> *Because you have done this, Cursed are you above all livestock and all wild animals! You will crawl on your belly and you will eat dust all the days of your life. And I will put enmity between you and the woman, and between your offspring and hers; he will crush your head, and you will strike his heel.*
> GENESIS 3:14–15 NIV

But that was just the first of literally hundreds of Old Testament prophecies about Jesus Christ. Over a period of several centuries, God continued to give prophetic visions and utterances that foretold the coming of the Savior.

Here are just a few of them:

- He would be born of a virgin (Isaiah 7:14; Luke 1:26–38)

- He would spend time in Egypt
  (Hosea 11:1; Matthew 2:14–15)

- He would be rejected by His own
  people (Psalm 69:8; Isaiah 53:3;
  John 1:11, 7:5)

- He would be declared the Son
  of God (Psalm 2:7; Matthew
  3:16–17)

- He would be betrayed (Psalm
  41:9; Zechariah 11:12–13; Luke
  22:47–48; Matthew 26:14–16)

- He would be falsely accused
  (Psalm 35:11; Mark 14:57–58)

- He would be hated for no reason
  (Psalm 35:19, John 15:24–25)

- He would arrive in Jerusalem on a
  donkey colt (Zechariah 9:9; Matthew 21:1–11)

- He would be crucified with criminals (Isaiah 53:12; Matthew 27:38)

- His hands and feet would be pierced (Psalm 22:16; John 20:25–27)

- He would be mocked and ridiculed (Psalm 22:7–8; Luke 23:35)

- He would be forsaken by God (Psalm 22:1; Matthew 27:46)

- He would be raised from the dead (Psalm 16:10, 49:15; Matthew 28:2–7)

- He would be a sacrifice for sin (Isaiah 53:5–12; Romans 5:6–8)

Jesus Christ didn't arrive on earth unannounced. On the contrary, the Savior's arrival—as well as the events surrounding His life, His teaching, His actions, and His death and resurrection—has been foretold for several centuries before His birth.

2. JESUS WAS GOD IN THE FLESH.

In the opening verse of his Gospel, the apostle John makes an astounding claim about the person of Jesus Christ: "In the beginning was the Word, and the Word was with God, and the Word was God" (John 1:1 KJV).

One of the pillars of the Christian faith is that the Savior, Jesus Christ, was at once a man and God, that He was God in the flesh: "And the Word was made flesh, and dwelt among us" (John 1:14 KJV).

During the course of His earthly ministry, Jesus repeated that very same claim about Himself:

- "Jesus answered, 'I tell you the truth, before Abraham was even born, I AM!'" (John 8:58 NLT).

- "I and the Father are one" (John 10:30 NIV).

- "He who has seen Me has seen the Father" (John 14:9 NASB).

- "Don't you believe that I am in the Father, and that the Father is in me? The words I say to you I do not speak on my own authority. Rather, it is the Father, living in me, who is doing his work" (John 14:10 NIV).

- "Now, Father, bring me into the glory we shared before the world began" (John 17:5 NLT).

Over the several decades after Jesus' death and resurrection, New Testament writers made many, many references to the divinity of Jesus, including:

- "Have the same mindset as Christ Jesus: Who, being in very nature God, did not consider equality with God something to be used to his own advantage" (Philippians 2:5–6 NIV).

- "For in Christ lives all the fullness of God in a human body" (Colossians 2:9 NLT).

- "He is the image of the invisible God, the firstborn over all creation. For by Him all things were created that are in heaven and that are on earth, visible and invisible, whether thrones or dominions or principalities or powers. All things were created through Him and for Him. And He is before all things, and in Him all things consist" (Colossians 1:15–17 NKJV).

- "...while we wait for the blessed hope—the appearing of the glory of our great God and Savior, Jesus Christ" (Titus 2:13 NIV).

- "But about the Son he says, 'Your throne, O God, will last for ever and ever; a scepter of justice will be the scepter of your kingdom'" (Hebrews 1:8 NIV).

- "On his robe and on his thigh he has this name written: KING OF KINGS AND LORD OF LORDS" (Revelation 19:16 NIV).

3. JESUS LIVED A SINLESS LIFE ON EARTH.

Jesus was unique among humans in that, though He lived life here on earth and was tempted to sin (see Matthew 4:1–11), He never once sinned in any way. The Bible says this about the life He led here on earth:

- "For God made Christ, who never sinned, to be the offering for our sin, so that we could be made right with God through Christ" (2 Corinthians 5:21 NLT).

- For we do not have a high priest who is unable to empathize with our weaknesses, but we have one who has been tempted in every way, just as we are—yet he did not sin" (Hebrews 4:15 NIV).

- He never sinned, nor ever deceived anyone. He did not retaliate when he was insulted, nor threaten revenge when he suffered. He left his case in the hands of God, who always judges fairly" (1 Peter 2:22–23 NLT).

But why is it important that Jesus—the One God sent to be the eternal sacrifice for the sins of all humankind—live a sinless life? The answer to that question can be found in the apostle Peter's first letter: "For you know that God paid a ransom to save you from the empty life you inherited from your ancestors. And the ransom he paid was not mere gold or silver. It was the precious blood of Christ, the sinless, spotless

Lamb of God" (1 Peter 1:18–19 NLT).

When Peter used the phrase "sinless, spotless Lamb of God," he was using terminology associated with Old Testament Law regarding animal sacrifices offered to God at the Passover to pay for sin. According to the Law, God required that a lamb sacrificed at the time of the Passover had to be a perfect specimen—without any kind of flaw on its skin, in its wool, or on its hooves (see Exodus 12:5). Before the lamb was sacrificed, it was penned up and examined thoroughly to make sure it was without any kind of blemish.

Jesus, the man of whom John the Baptist said, "Behold! The Lamb of God who takes away the sin of the world!" (John 1:29 NKJV) was likewise perfect. He lived on earth for thirty-three years, never allowing Himself to become flawed or stained with any kind of sin. He was absolutely perfect in His behavior, in His words, and in His thoughts. And when the time was right, He gave Himself up as the one and only acceptable sacrifice for our sins.

4. JESUS SHED HIS BLOOD FOR US.

The New Testament is filled with references to Jesus shedding His blood so that sinners could find forgiveness for their wrongdoing.

But why did Jesus have to shed His blood?

First of all, the Bible teaches that sin always requires a sacrifice. The writer of the book of Hebrews pointed out, "In fact, the law requires that nearly everything be cleansed with blood, and without the shedding of blood there is no forgiveness" (Hebrews 9:22 NIV).

Why did Jesus have to shed His blood?

Under Old Testament Law, people were required to sacrifice the life of an innocent animal in order to atone for their sin (see Leviticus 17:11). But these sacrifices were imperfect in that they had to be repeated because they were merely a foreshadowing of the perfect sacrifice of Jesus Christ on the cross (see Hebrews 10:1–4).

According to the Gospel of John, Jesus' final words from the cross, just before He drew His last breath, were, "It is finished" (John 19:30). By shedding His blood and dying on a wooden cross, Jesus had completed the final sacrifice for the sins of the world. No longer would people need to sacrifice animals to cover their sins against God. Jesus had paid the ultimate price, providing the forgiveness of sin.

The Bible teaches that Christ's shed blood provides those who believe in Him many wonderful benefits:

- It established the "New Covenant"—a new relationship between God and humans based not on Old Testament Law but on the sacrificial death of Jesus Christ (Matthew 26:28; Mark 14:24; Luke 22:20; Romans 3:23–25; 1 Corinthians 11:25; Hebrews 9:12).

- It cleanses us from sin and gives us forgiveness and a clean conscience (Hebrews 9:14, 9:22, 13:10–12; 1 John 1:7; Revelation 7:14).

- It justifies us before God (Romans 5:8–10).

- It frees us from slavery to sin (Ephesians 1:7; 1 Peter 1:18–19; Revelation 1:5–6, 5:9).

- It gives us spiritual life (John 6:53–56; 1 Corinthians 10:16).

- It reconciles us to God (Ephesians 2:13; Colossians 1:20).

- It gives us confidence and assurance before God (Hebrews 10:19, 12:24).

- It defeats the devil and his work (Revelation 12:11).

5. JESUS WAS RAISED FROM THE DEAD. All four Gospels—the New Testament books that tell the story of Jesus' birth, life, works, teachings, and death—include the final, pivotal chapter of Jesus' earthly ministry: His resurrection from the dead

and His ascension back to heaven.

Before His death, Jesus had promised His disciples that while He would have to suffer and die, He would be miraculously raised from the dead three days later:

> *Now Jesus was going up to Jerusalem. On the way, he took the Twelve aside and said to them, 'We are going up to Jerusalem, and the Son of Man will be delivered over to the chief priests and the teachers of the law. They will condemn him to death and will hand him over to the Gentiles to be mocked and flogged and crucified. On the third day he will be raised to life!(Matthew 20:17–19 niv; also see Mark 10:33–34, Luke 18:31–33).*

True to His promise, Jesus did suffer and die on a cross and was resurrected on the third day after His death (see Matthew 28:2–20; Mark 16; Luke 24; John 20:1–21:6).

The apostle Paul pointed out the fundamental importance of Jesus' resurrection when he wrote:

And if Christ has not been raised, then all our preaching is useless, and your faith is useless. And we apostles would all be lying about God—for we have said that God raised Christ from the grave. But that can't be true if there is no resurrection of the dead. And if there is no resurrection of the dead, then Christ has not been raised. And if Christ has not been raised, then your faith is useless and you are still guilty of your sins.

1 CORINTHIANS 15:14–17 NLT

Without the resurrection of Jesus from the dead, the Christian faith would be at best worthless and at worst a giant deception that would leave sinners lost and on their way to eternal punishment. The Old Testament predicted this event, and Jesus promised it would take place on the third day after His death. Had it not happened, then we could put no trust in anything the Old Testament prophets, Jesus, or the New Testament writers have told us.

But Jesus was raised from the dead. The Bible reports this event and backs it up with several dependable eyewitness accounts (see 1 Corinthians 15:3–8). And because God raised Jesus from the dead, we too can be brought from spiritual death to spiritual life through Him.

6. JESUS RETURNED TO HEAVEN TO TAKE HIS PLACE WITH HIS FATHER.

In the days and weeks following His resurrection, Jesus continued His earthly ministry—appearing to the women who followed Him (Matthew 28:9–10), to His apostles (Luke 24:36–43), and to more than five hundred others of His followers.

Then came the day when His earthly ministry was finished, the day He returned to heaven. Jesus had successfully accomplished everything the Father had sent Him to do, so He took His disciples to a place near Jerusalem called Mount Olivet. There He gave them some final instructions, promised them the arrival of the

Holy Spirit, and blessed them. Then He was "taken up before their very eyes, and a cloud hid him from their sight" (Acts 1:9 NIV). Moments later, two angels appeared to the disciples, telling them that Jesus would return one day "in the same way you have seen him go into heaven" (vs. 11).

In the meantime, the Bible teaches, Jesus is seated "in the place of honor beside the throne of the majestic God in heaven. There he ministers in the heavenly Tabernacle, the true place of worship that was built by the Lord and not by human hands" (Hebrews 8:1-2 NLT).

Jesus' return to heaven is important for several reasons:

- It marked the time when He could fulfill His promise to send the Holy Spirit to live within every believer (see John 16:5–15).

- It put Him in position to intercede with God on behalf of every believer (see Hebrews 7:25).

It put Him in a place where He could stand in the gap as our advocate with God when we sin (see 1 John 2:1–2).

- He is in heaven, preparing an eternal home for all who believe in Him (John 14:1–3).

God looked through the lens of eternity and identified something that He knew humans, His most prized and loved creation, desperately needed: a Savior to take away their sins and bring them into fellowship with Him. And as He worked to bring that Savior into the world, He made sure to let us know that the one and only Savior He had provided was everything we needed.

GOD'S "EXCLUSIVE/INCLUSIVE" SALVATION MESSAGE

A legendary story about the great twentieth-century comedian W.C. Fields, notorious for his drinking, womanizing, and agnosticism, reflects an attitude among many who deny or question the biblical teaching that faith in Jesus Christ is the only way to eternal salvation. As Fields lay on his death bed, he was caught reading the Bible. When someone asked him why he was reading the Book he'd ignored all his life, he replied, "I'm looking for a loophole."

There can be no doubt that W.C. never found that loophole. The Bible teaches that all humans are sinners and that there is but one way to receive forgiveness for our sins and to gain entrance into God's eternal kingdom.

God's message of salvation is very exclusive in that He has provided only one way to eternal life: Jesus Christ. But it is also very inclusive in that He has offered the free gift

> God has provided only one way to eternal life: Jesus Christ.

of salvation to anyone who will simply accept it in faith:

- "And it will come about that whoever calls on the name of the LORD will be delivered" (Joel 2:32 NASB).

- "Yet to all who did receive him, to those who believed in his name, he gave the right to become children of God" (John 1:12 NIV).

- "For God loved the world so much that he gave his one and only Son, so that everyone who believes in him will not perish but have eternal life. God sent his Son into the world not to judge the world, but to save the world through him" (John 3:16–17 NLT).

- "I now realize how true it is that God does not show favoritism but accepts from every nation the one who fears him and does what is right" (Acts 10:34–35 NIV).

- "If you confess with your mouth Jesus as Lord, and believe in your heart that God raised Him from the dead, you will be saved" (Romans 10:9 NASB).

- "He is the atoning sacrifice for our sins, and not only for ours but also for the sins of the whole world" (1 John 2:2 NIV).

- "For the grace of God has been revealed, bringing salvation to all people" (Titus 2:11 NLT).

- "The Lord isn't really being slow about his promise, as some people think. No, he is being patient for your sake. He does not want anyone to be destroyed, but wants everyone to repent" (2 Peter 3:9 NLT).

- "The Spirit and the bride say, 'Come!' And let the one who hears say, 'Come!' Let the one who is thirsty come; and let the one who wishes take the free gift of the water of life" (Revelation 22:17 NIV).

God's invitation to receive the free gift of salvation is open to all people, but it has to be on His terms, not ours. There is only one way to peace with God, forgiveness of sins, and eternal salvation, and it's through the Savior that God has provided—Jesus Christ.

This leaves each and every one of us facing the most important question we will ever answer: *What will we do with the Savior?*

4
WHAT MUST I DO...?

"Sirs, what must I do to be saved?"

An unnamed Philippian jailer—a prison guard, in modern terms—had a lot on his mind. He had been assigned the job of guarding a prison in which the apostle Paul and his traveling companion Silas had been bound up in chains after their preaching had caused some serious financial problems for a prominent slave owner living in the ancient city of Philippi.

Just moments before, the jailer had drawn his own sword, intending to commit suicide after a violent earthquake had released Paul and Silas—and the other prisoners—from their chains and caused the prison doors to fly open. He was sure the prisoners had taken advantage of an unexpected opportunity to escape, and he so feared the consequences of failing to keep his prisoners in their cells that he saw self-inflicted death as the better of two equally horrible alternatives.

But Paul and Silas hadn't gone anywhere. Sensing that the guard was about to commit suicide, Paul called out from the cell, urging him not to harm himself because the prisoners were still in the jail.

It's hard to say what made a bigger impression on this guard: the fact that Paul and Silas prayed and sang to God after being beaten and jailed, or that they stayed in their cell when they could just as easily have made a quick getaway from the jail *and* the city.

After witnessing a miracle and an amazing act of compassion on the part of those he had been assigned to guard—and after feeling what had to be an overwhelming sense of relief that he wasn't about to violently lose his life at the hands of his superiors—this man turned his attention to another issue: his eternal destiny.

This jailer knew he needed a savior, and he had become convinced that Paul and Silas had what he needed. After rushing into the prison and throwing himself at the apostles' feet, he brought them both outside the prison cell and asked the question millions have asked, and continue to ask, ever since:

"What must I do to be saved?"

"Sirs, what must I do to be saved?" (Acts 16:30 NIV).

The Bible doesn't tell us what kind of answer this jailer expected, only that he asked a very sincere and very important question. But had he been like many people living today, he might have expected Paul and Silas to present him with a long list of conditions for eternal salvation:

"Make sure you follow every rule and law written in the Old Testament."

"Always treat people fairly and justly, even when they don't treat you the same way."

"Never lose your temper, and never think or speak badly of anyone."

"Go to synagogue every Sabbath Day,

and absolutely never do any work of any kind on that day."

"Give a part of your income to helping the poor."

But Paul and Silas didn't make any mention of rules to follow or deeds to do. Instead, they delivered a simple message of God's one condition for eternal salvation: "Believe in the Lord Jesus, and you will be saved—you and your household." (Acts 16:31 NIV).

That was the greatest news that Philippian jailer could have heard. And it's the same Good News God has for us today.

SALVATION: IT'S ALL ABOUT FAITH

If there is one word that can best describe Christianity, it is probably *faith*. The writer of Hebrews underscored the vital importance of faith when he wrote, "And without faith it is impossible to please God, because anyone who comes to him must believe that he exists and that he rewards those who earnestly seek him" (11:6 NIV).

No matter what we do, no matter how hard we try, no matter how sincere and well-intentioned we may be, nothing we do will please God unless it is done with a heart attitude of faith—faith that God really is, that He loves us, and that He wants to freely give us His very best.

His very best. When God sent Jesus into the world to live a perfect life of faith and to die a sacrificial death for our sins, He was giving us the very best He has. And

> If we want the wonderful gift of salvation Jesus offers, we have to receive it by faith.

if we want the wonderful gift of salvation Jesus offers, we have to receive it by faith.

The New Testament is filled with references to the wonderful message of salvation through faith—through truly believing in and relying on the Lord Jesus Christ. But this promise didn't suddenly appear with the arrival of Jesus Christ or with the start of the New Testament church. On the contrary, the first biblical mention of what Bible scholars and theologians call "justification through faith" appears in the book of Genesis: "Abram believed the LORD, and he credited it to him as righteousness" (Genesis 15:6 NIV).

Abraham (he was known as Abram early on in his walk of faith) was one of the Old Testament figures who played a key role in the foundation of the nation of Israel and in God's fulfilling His plan to bring the Savior into the world. And, like him, we today are saved through faith.

The New Testament is filled with verses and passages teaching the truth of salvation through faith. Jesus Himself stated on several occasions that people would be saved through believing in Him:

- "And as Moses lifted up the bronze snake on a pole in the wilderness, so the Son of Man must be lifted up, so that everyone who believes in him will have eternal life" (John 3:14–15 NLT).

- "For God so loved the world, that he gave his only begotten Son, that whosoever believeth in him should not perish, but have everlasting life" (John 3:16 KJV).

- "Whoever believes in the Son has eternal life, but whoever rejects the Son will not see life, for God's wrath remains on them" (John 3:36 NIV).

- "Very truly I tell you, whoever hears my word and believes him who sent me has eternal life and will not be judged but has crossed over from death to life" (John 5:24 NIV).

- "Then they said to Him, 'What shall we do, that we may work the works of God?' Jesus answered and said to them, 'This is the work of God, that you believe in Him whom He sent'" (John 6:28–29 NKJV).

- "I am the resurrection and the life. He who believes in Me, though he may die, he shall live. And whoever lives and believes in Me shall never die" (John 11:25–26 NKJV).

Jesus, whom the writer of Hebrews called "the author and finisher of our faith" (12:2), had a lot to say about salvation through faith, and other New Testament figures and writers placed faith at the center of the message God had sent them to proclaim:

- "Believe on the Lord Jesus Christ, and thou shalt be saved" (Acts 16:31 KJV).

- "Even the righteousness of God which is by faith of Jesus Christ unto all and upon all them that believe: for there is no difference" (Romans 3:22 KJV).

- "God presented Christ as a sacrifice of atonement, through the shedding of his blood—to be received by faith" (Romans 3:25 NIV).

- "He did it to demonstrate his righteousness at the present time, so as to be just and the one who justifies those who have faith in Jesus" (Romans 3:26 NIV).

- "For the Scriptures tell us, 'Abraham believed God, and God counted him as righteous because of his faith'" (Romans 4:3 NLT).

- "He [Abraham] received the sign of circumcision, a seal of the righteousness of the faith which he had while uncircumcised, so that he might be the father of all who believe without being circumcised, that righteousness might be credited to them" (Romans 4:11 NASB).

- "Therefore being justified by faith, we have peace with God through our Lord Jesus Christ: By whom also we have access by faith into this grace wherein we stand, and rejoice in hope of the glory of God" (Romans 5:1–2 KJV).

- "What shall we say then? That the Gentiles, which followed not after righteousness, have attained to righteousness, even the righteousness which is of faith" (Romans 9:30 KJV).

- "As it is written: 'See, I lay in Zion a stone that causes people to stumble and a rock that makes them fall, and the one who believes in him will never be put to shame'" (Romans 9:33 NIV).

- "If you confess with your mouth the Lord Jesus and believe in your heart that God has raised Him from the dead, you will be saved. For with the heart one believes unto righteousness, and with the mouth confession is made unto salvation" (Romans 10:9–10 NKJV).

- "For the Scripture says, 'Whoever believes on Him will not be put to shame'" (Romans 10:11 NKJV).

- "Scripture foresaw that God would justify the Gentiles by faith, and announced the gospel in advance to Abraham: 'All nations will be blessed through you.' So those who rely on faith are blessed along with Abraham, the man of faith" (Galatians 3:8–9 NIV).

- "He redeemed us in order that the blessing given to Abraham might come to the Gentiles through Christ Jesus, so that by faith we might receive the promise of the Spirit" (Galatians 3:14 NIV).

- "But Scripture has locked up everything under the control of sin, so that what was promised, being given through faith in Jesus Christ, might be given to those who believe" (Galatians 3:22 NIV).

- "In whom ye also trusted, after that ye heard the word of truth, the gospel of your salvation: in whom also after that ye believed, ye were sealed with that holy Spirit of promise" (Ephesians 1:13 KJV).

- "However, for this reason I obtained mercy, that in me first Jesus Christ might show all longsuffering, as a pattern to those who are going to believe on Him for everlasting life" (1 Timothy 1:16 NKJV).

- "Though you have not seen him, you love him; and even though you do not see him now, you believe in him and are filled with an inexpressible and glorious joy, for you are receiving the end result of your faith, the salvation of your souls" (1 Peter 1:8–9 NIV).

- "Whosoever believeth that Jesus is the Christ is born of God" (1 John 5:1 KJV).

- "And this is the testimony: God has given us eternal life, and this life is in his Son. Whoever has the Son has life; whoever does not have the Son of God does not have life. I write these things to you who believe in the name of the Son of God so that you may know that you have eternal life" (1 John 5:11–13 NIV).

SALVATION THROUGH FAITH AND...?

After reading the list of passages above, it should be abundantly clear that salvation comes through faith, and not through anything we can possibly do.

There is, however, a passage in the New Testament that, at least at first glance, seems to indicate that people are saved on the basis not just of faith but also on the basis of the good things they do for others. The apostle James penned these troublesome words:

> *What good is it, my brothers and sisters, if someone claims to have faith but has no deeds? Can such faith save them? Suppose a brother or a sister is without clothes and daily food. If one of you says to them, "Go in peace; keep warm and well fed," but does nothing about their physical needs, what good is it? In the same way, faith by itself, if it is not accompanied by action, is dead.*
> JAMES 2:14–17 NIV

James further muddies the waters (again, at first glance) when he goes on to write, "You see that a person is considered righteous by what they do and not by faith alone" (vs. 24).

James's words seem at first a direct contradiction to the many scripture verses that spell out very clearly that we are justified before God (saved) though faith in Christ alone. He seems to be saying that no one can be saved unless they do good deeds. Is that a contradiction?

Actually, there is no contradiction at all between the writings of James and the many passages teaching salvation by faith in Christ alone. James was merely pointing out that there will be a cause-and-effect process in the life of a person who has true faith in Jesus. In other words, if you have a genuine, living faith in Christ, that faith will demonstrate

> If you have a genuine, living faith in Christ, that faith will demonstrate itself in how you live.

115

itself in how you live, how you think, and how you treat others.

Jesus taught His disciples essentially the same thing in the parable of the sheep and the goats:

> *Then the King will say to those on his right, "Come, you who are blessed by my Father; take your inheritance, the kingdom prepared for you since the creation of the world. For I was hungry and you gave me something to eat, I was thirsty and you gave me something to drink, I was a stranger and you invited me in, I needed clothes and you clothed me, I was sick and you looked after me, I was in prison and you came to visit me." "Then the righteous will answer him, Lord, when did we see you hungry and feed you, or thirsty and give you something to drink? When did we see you a stranger and invite you in, or needing clothes and clothe you? When did we see you sick or in prison and*

> *go to visit you?" The King will reply,*
> *"Truly I tell you, whatever you did*
> *for one of the least of these brothers*
> *and sisters of mine, you did for me."*
> MATTHEW 25:34–40 NIV

If you take this passage by itself, it seems Jesus is telling His followers that they could be saved through their acts of kindness—through giving the poor and needy housing, food, drink, and clothing. But if you look at this parable in the light of other scripture—including the words of Jesus Himself in the passage listed earlier in this chapter—you will see that we are saved through the work of the Savior, not by acts of kindness and charity to others.

James wanted his readers to understand the difference between a living, growing faith and a dead faith. The living faith shows itself through a changed life and good works—while a dead faith doesn't change anything.

The Bible is clear: Our salvation has

nothing to do with our own merit or anything we've done. It has everything to do with God's compassionate mercy. But the Bible is also clear that "if anyone is in Christ, he is a new creation; old things have passed away; behold, all things have become new" (2 Corinthians 5:17 NKJV). This simply means that when we come to faith in Christ, we are saved *and* changed—changed in how we think, in how we behave, and in how we relate to other people. When we come to faith in Jesus, we turn from our old lives and old ways of thinking to an entirely new experience—including good works.

> When we come to faith in Christ, we are changed in how we think, in how we behave, and in how we relate to other people.

To put it simply, we are not saved *because* of our new thinking and good works; we engage in new thinking and good works because we are saved through the work of our Savior.

THE REWARDS OF FAITH—
ETERNAL AND OTHERWISE

When you read words such as *faith* or *belief* in the Bible, they usually refer to one of two things: the faith or belief leading to eternal salvation or the faith or belief needed to live a life that pleases God—and to accomplish great things for God.

The Bible lists several wonderful things God does for us when we simply believe Him and receive His promise of salvation through faith in Jesus Christ. Through this kind of faith, we are:

- *Justified (made right with God)*—
  "Through him everyone who believes is set free from every sin, a justification you were not able to obtain under the law of Moses" (Acts 13:39 NIV; also see Romans 3:21–22, 28, 30; Galatians 2:16).

- *Saved from eternal condemnation*—
  "Whoever believes and is baptized will be saved, but whoever does

not believe will be condemned" (Mark 16:16 NIV; also see Acts 16:31).

- *Brought into spiritual light*— "Believe in the light while you have the light, so that you may become children of light. . . . I have come into the world as a light, so that no one who believes in me should stay in darkness" (John 12:36, 46 NIV).

- *Given spiritual life*—"But these are written, that ye might believe that Jesus is the Christ, the Son of God; and that believing ye might have life through his name" (John 20:31 KJV; also see Galatians 2:20).

- *Given eternal life*—"Whoever believes in Him should not perish but have eternal life. For God so loved the world that He gave His only begotten Son, that whoever believes in Him should not perish but have everlasting life" (John 3:15–16 NKJV; also see John 6:40, 47).

- *Given eternal rest*—"Now we who have believed enter that rest, just as God has said, 'So I declared on oath in my anger, "They shall never enter my rest."' And yet his works have been finished since the creation of the world" (Hebrews 4:3 NIV).

- *Preserved for eternal salvation*—". . .who are protected by the power of God through faith for a salvation ready to be revealed in the last time" (1 Peter 1:5 NASB).

- *Adopted into God's family*—"But as many as received Him, to them He gave the right to become children of God, even to those who believe in His name" (John 1:12 NASB; also see Galatians 3:26).

- *Given access to God*—"In him and through faith in him we may approach God with freedom and confidence" (Ephesians 3:12 NIV).

- *Made recipients of everything God has promised*—"But the Scripture has confined all under sin, that the promise by faith in Jesus Christ might be given to those who believe" (Galatians 3:22 NKJV).

- *Given God's Holy Spirit*—"And as I began to speak, the Holy Spirit fell upon them just as He did upon us at the beginning. And I remembered the word of the Lord, how He used to say, 'John baptized with water, but you will be baptized with the Holy Spirit.' Therefore if God gave to them the same gift as He gave to us also after believing in the Lord Jesus Christ, who was I that I could stand in God's way?" (Acts 11:15–17

NASB; also see Galatians 3:14;
Ephesians 1:13).

When we think of the word *saved* in
the spiritual context, we usually associate
it with being rescued from eternal punishment after we die. But, as you can see in
the passages you just read, God has so much
more in store for those who have received
eternal salvation by faith.

CLOTHED IN CHRIST'S RIGHTEOUSNESS. . .THROUGH FAITH

In chapters 1 and 2 of this book, you read
about how all humans born after the fall
of Adam and Eve (with the exception of
Jesus Christ) are sinners and are utterly
incapable of living a truly righteous life,
which is God's one standard.

The truth is that, without God's own
intervention, we are doomed. The Bible
tells us that the very best we have to offer God in terms of righteous living can
be likened to "filthy rags" (see Isaiah 64:6).

No matter how hard we try not to offend God in what we say, do, or think, no matter how many good things we do in an effort to please Him, we can never meet God's standard of sinless perfection.

We find that no matter how hard we try, we can't love God and others more than we love ourselves, can't completely rid ourselves of impure or inappropriate thoughts, and can't completely stop doing the things we know God doesn't approve of. Our sinful nature taints everything we do, everything we say, and everything we think. Yet God requires that we live a life free of sin if we want to go to heaven for all eternity.

> No matter how hard we try, we can't love God and others more than we love ourselves.

This is where what theologians call "imputed righteousness" comes into the picture. In this context, the word *impute* means to accredit or attribute something to someone, even if it hasn't been earned or isn't necessarily deserved.

In layman's terms, imputed righteousness is the process whereby God attributes or credits people with the righteousness of His Son, who was the only man ever to live a perfectly sinless life. Another way to describe imputed righteousness is to say that when God looks at the one who trusts Jesus Christ for salvation, He chooses not to see that person's sin but instead sees the righteousness of Christ in that person.

Amazingly, that is not the end of the story of imputed righteousness. You see, not only does God impute Christ's righteousness to us through faith, He also imputes our sin to His one and only Son. That is what the Bible means when it says, "God made him who had no sin to be sin for us, so that in him we might become the righteousness of God" (2 Corinthians 5:21 NIV).

Jesus' life here on earth was marked by perfect obedience to His heavenly Father. He was perfect in everything He did, everything He said, and everything He thought. At no point did He do anything that displeased God, and at no point did He fail to do what the Father required Him to do.

That includes willingly giving Himself up to die a sacrificial death on a wooden cross. As the apostle Paul wrote, "Though he was God, he did not think of equality with God as something to cling to. Instead, he gave up his divine privileges; he took the humble position of a slave and was born as a human being. When he appeared in human form, he humbled himself in obedience to God and died a criminal's death on a cross" (Philippians 2:6–8 NLT).

> When we come to Jesus in faith, God intentionally sees His righteousness instead of our sin.

Paul also wrote, "Blessed is the man to whom the Lord will not *impute* sin" (Romans 4:8 KJV, italics added). That is the greatest blessing we can receive when we place our faith in the saving work of Jesus Christ. When we come to Jesus in faith, God intentionally sees His righteousness instead of our sin.

So what must you do to be saved? It's as

simple as coming to God in faith, confessing your own sinfulness, acknowledging that you need the Savior, and receiving the free gift of salvation through Jesus Christ. When you do that, you begin a new life of faith and forgiveness—as well as a place in God's eternal kingdom.

And you'll never be the same!

5
SOME FAQS ABOUT OUR NEED FOR THE SAVIOR

Up to this point in this book, you've read about why we humans need a Savior—more specifically *the* Savior, Jesus Christ. You've also read about how God provided the Savior for you as a perfect once-and-for all sacrifice for your sin.

Now, if you'll read on for just a few more pages, you will see some answers to some of the questions so many people ask about the Savior and what He desires from you.

Q—Why did Jesus have to die for our sins?

A—As you read in chapter 1 of this book, God had warned Adam and Eve that if they disobeyed in the one small command He had given them, then they "would surely die" (Genesis 2:17). When the world's first two human beings chose to disobey God, they had to be punished—along with the rest of humanity because all of us are guilty of violating God's holy standards (see Romans 3:23).

The Bible identifies God as love personified (1 John 4:8), but it also identifies Him as a holy and perfect God who cannot tolerate or overlook sin. The consequences of sin are simple but terrible. As the apostle Paul wrote, "The wages of sin is death" (Romans 6:23). That means that without God's own intervention, every human being who followed Adam and Eve would have to die for their sins.

As we pointed out earlier in this book, neither Adam nor Eve died physically on the very day they rebelled against God. In fact, both of them lived for hundreds of years after the day of "the Fall." But on that day, they died in the most important way a human can die: spiritually. God banished them from the Garden of Eden, which was a picture of perfect fellowship with the Creator. Sin had separated Adam and Eve from God, and sin has separated each of us from Him ever since.

But God didn't leave Adam and Eve, or the rest of us, without hope. On the day they sinned, God announced that He would send the Messiah, the Savior, to pay the price for what they had done (see Genesis 3:15). In His never-ending love for humanity, God immediately began bringing about His plan to give the greatest gift of love ever given. God had a promise to keep, and He reaffirmed that promise to men such as Abraham, Moses, and David, and He also used great prophets such as Isaiah, Jeremiah, Daniel, and many others to announce the coming of the Savior.

> God didn't leave Adam and Eve, or the rest of us, without hope.

Yes, the Messiah would come one day. But in the meantime, people offered imperfect sacrifices on earthen altars to atone for their sins. While God didn't excuse or overlook sin, He allowed people to demonstrate their sorrow over their wrongdoing—and to escape eternal punishment—by offering the best they had available to them.

But that system of sacrifices and atonement was just a foreshadowing of the one perfect sin sacrifice—the One God Himself would provide when the time was right. Once all the preparations had been made, God sent His one and only Son, Jesus Christ, into the world to live a perfect life and die a sacrificial death so that people could be reconciled to their Creator.

God's holiness and perfection required that He punish all sin, but His amazing love motivated Him to lay the punishment for every sin that has ever been committed on His own beloved Son, the only man in human history to live a completely sinless life: "God made him who had no sin to be sin for us, so that in him we might become the righteousness of God" (2 Corinthians 5:21 NIV).

Jesus had to die for our sins because His Father, a righteous God, can never let sin go unpunished. The Bible teaches that God sent His Son into the world to take the punishment for our sins so that we could be put in good standing with Him:

> *For everyone has sinned; we all fall short of God's glorious standard. Yet God, with undeserved kindness, declares that we are righteous. He did this through Christ Jesus when he freed us from the penalty for our sins. For God presented Jesus as the sacrifice for sin. People are made right with God when they believe that Jesus sacrificed his life, shedding his blood.*
> ROMANS 3:23–25 NLT

Humanly speaking, it doesn't seem quite fair that the one man who lived a perfect life should have to suffer and die on a cross in place of a sinful and lost human race, does it? But if you want to put it in terms like "fair," then each of us deserves to die for our own sins. That is, after all, the debt each of us owes for the evil we have done and the good we have failed to do.

As a holy and just God, our Creator knew from the very beginning that we each deserve to die for our sin. But as a loving and kind heavenly Father, He did what only He could do, what we didn't deserve, when He made the one perfect sacrifice that would pay for the sins of the entire world (see 1 John 2:2).

Q—I have surrendered my life to Jesus Christ, and He has made a lot of huge changes in me. So why do I still sin—in my thoughts and in my actions? As hard as I try, I still do things, say things, and think things I know aren't pleasing to God. What is my problem?

A—There are, unfortunately, several "movements" within Christianity today teaching that believers can achieve sinless perfection here and now, in this world. One of the unintended consequences of this kind of teaching (and it is not based in any sound reading of the Bible) is self-condemnation and a crippling sense of guilt on the part of Christians who recognize their own sinfulness or who struggle with certain sins.

The Bible has a lot to say about who and what believers in and followers of Christ really are. It calls us "saints," "God's children," "citizens of heaven," and many other titles that underscore the promises God has made those who have acknowledged their need for the Savior and who have placed their faith in Him. But nowhere does it tell us that we will be sinless, perfect human beings here on earth.

Even the apostle Paul—the man God chose to preach the message of the Savior to the Gentile (non-Jewish) world of his day—had his share of struggles with sin, which he shared openly with the church in Rome:

> *The trouble is with me, for I am all too human, a slave to sin. I don't really understand myself, for I want to do what is right, but I don't do it. Instead, I do what I hate. But if I know that what I am doing is wrong, this shows that I agree that the law is good. So I am not the one doing wrong; it is sin living in me that does it. And I know that nothing good lives in me, that is, in my sinful nature. I want to do what is right, but I can't. I want to do what is good, but I don't. I don't want to do what is wrong, but I do it anyway. But if I do what I don't want to do, I am not really the one doing wrong; it is sin living in me that does it.*
>
> ROMANS 7:14–20 NLT

Paul was acknowledging something all Christians need to understand, and it's this: While God loves us and has called us His own people, while we still live in this earth we will struggle with the sinful nature all people possess. And while God has promised us ultimate victory over sin, we will still struggle with sin (in one way or another) for the remainder of our lives on earth.

> While we still live in this earth we will struggle with the sinful nature all people possess.

Some people, including many Christians, fall into the trap of believing that God is just waiting in heaven for them to mess up so He can drop the hammer—or worse, completely give up on them. But it doesn't work that way. As much as the devil wants us to believe that God stops loving us when we fall, He has promised never to give up on us and to do everything He can to give us victory over sin.

When you sin, remember these important, Bible-based facts:

- Your own sin should serve as
  a reminder of just how much
  you need the Savior (see 1 John
  4:9–10).

- While God loves you enough to
  correct you and discipline you for
  your sin (see Hebrews 12:5–11),
  He will not condemn you when
  you fall: "There is now no condemnation for those who are in
  Christ Jesus" (Romans 8:1 NIV).

- He will forgive and cleanse you
  when you confess your sin: "If
  we confess our sins, he is faithful
  and just and will forgive us our
  sins and purify us from all unrigh-
  teousness" (1 John 1:9 NIV). Faithful and just—that means God will
  never break His promise to forgive
  you and cleanse you when you
  come to Him to confess your sins.

- You are forgiven—completely forgiven: "Praise the LORD, my soul, and forget not all his benefits—who forgives all your sins and heals all your diseases (Psalm 103:2–3 NIV).

- God has promised to finish what He has started in you: ". . .being confident of this, that he who began a good work in you will carry it on to completion until the day of Christ Jesus" (Philippians 1:6 NIV).

This side of heaven, none of us will ever achieve sinless perfection. But we have the privilege of being honest with God about the things we do, say, and think that are not pleasing to Him. When God's Holy Spirit lets us know where we are falling short, we can confess our sins to Him and then repent—meaning change our attitudes and actions.

Q—How do I convince a good person— someone who lives a good life of integrity and compassion—that he needs the Savior?

A—First of all, it's not your job to "convince" anyone that he or she needs the Savior. The Bible says that it is your job to live a life that pleases God and brings glory to Him (Matthew 5:16), tell others about Jesus (Acts 1:8), and be ready to let people know that Jesus is the reason for the hope you have within you (1 Peter 3:15).

The Bible tells us that it is ultimately God Himself, not us, who brings people to Jesus (see John 6:44–45). Your part in that equation is to do the things listed above and to pray that God would touch people around you with His Holy Spirit. When you feel a burden for someone you know needs the Savior, it is often because God is prompting you to pray for that person. Pray consistently, pray daily, and pray specifically. Don't just pray special blessings on the people you know need the Savior; pray that God's Spirit will touch the hearts and minds of the lost people you care about and show them that they need Jesus.

Q—What can I say to someone who believes he's done too many terrible things for God to ever forgive him?

A—The devil will use any tactic at his disposal to keep people from receiving the grace and forgiveness of sin God has so freely offered. One of his favorite tactics is to focus our attention on the worst sins we have committed and whisper the lie, "There is no way God can ever forgive you for *that*."

Most of us have little trouble believing that God will forgive "smaller" sins such as outbursts of anger, lying, foul language, and lustful thoughts. But when it comes to the "biggies"—murder, adultery, and others—some of us aren't so sure that God can, or even wants to, forgive *that* kind of sinner.

At issue here isn't the size of the sin,

but the depth of God's love and the power of the blood of Christ to cover any wrongdoing we confess to Him. There truly is no sin so terrible that God can't forgive it. And when a person—even the very worst of sinners—places his or her faith in the Savior, those sins are washed away, never again to be held against him or her.

If you'd like a biblical example of God's forgiveness of what we'd consider the worst of sins, then take a look at King David, who tried to cover one sin (adultery) by committing another (murder). Though David and his family paid a heavy price for his misdeeds, God forgave David and restored the king to fellowship with Himself (see 2 Samuel 11–12).

There is only one sin that God will not—cannot—forgive, and that is the sin of refusing to acknowledge that you need the Savior and receive the forgiveness that is found only in Jesus Christ. A person

> There is only one sin that God will not—cannot—forgive.

141

may have done some of the worst things we can imagine, but God is ready and able to forgive him or her—no matter what he or she has done in the past.

Jesus promised, "whoever comes to me I will never drive away" (John 6:37). Jesus didn't add a qualifier to His "whoever," but instead promised that He would receive whoever comes to Him—no matter what they've done in the past.

Q—Do I need to get my act together or clean up my life before I can come to Christ?

A—A lot of people—even many who know they need the Savior—make the mistake of thinking they need to break bad habits, stop certain sins, or make amends with other people before they are "good enough" to come to Christ for salvation.

That kind of thinking is, for lack of a better term, backwards and completely wrong.

Remember, in earlier chapters of this book, we explained how all human beings born since Adam and Eve (with the exception of Jesus Christ) are sinners who need the Savior. We also pointed out that the Bible teaches that no one is able to do anything to "save" himself or herself other than trusting in Jesus Christ.

And if there is nothing we can do to save ourselves or make ourselves "good enough" for God, then it only stands to reason that we come

> We come to the Savior just the way we are and let Him do the cleansing.

to the Savior just the way we are and let *Him* do the cleansing and forgiving.

The classic old hymn puts it this way:

> *Just as I am, without one plea,*
> *But that Thy blood was shed for me,*
> *And that Thou bidst me come to Thee,*
> *O Lamb of God, I come, I come.*

When God shows a person that he or she is a sinner and needs the Savior, it isn't an invitation for that person to "get it together" or "clean up his act"—on the contrary, it's an invitation to come to Jesus Christ.

Q—What should I say to a person who wants to put off salvation, to "live a little" before becoming a Christian?

A—A lot of people, especially the young, make the mistake of thinking that they have a long life ahead of them and that they will be able to turn to the Savior somewhere down the road. But common sense—and a little observation—shows us that there are no guarantees of a long life for anyone. People die unexpectedly, and for a variety of reasons—from sudden illnesses, from accidents, and from the actions of others.

The Bible contains hundreds of wonderful promises, but among them is not a guarantee of a certain number of years, weeks, or days of life here on earth. On the contrary, it warns us that our lives are brief and that only

God knows how long we will live:

- "LORD, remind me how brief my
  time on earth will be. Remind
  me that my days are numbered,
  and that my life is fleeing
  away. My life is no longer than
  the width of my hand. An entire
  lifetime is just a moment to you;
  human existence is but a breath"
  (Psalm 39:4–5 NLT).

- "Why, you do not even know what
  will happen tomorrow. What is
  your life? You are a mist that appears for a little while and then
  vanishes" (James 4:14 NIV).

- "A person's days are determined;
  you have decreed the number of
  his months and have set limits he
  cannot exceed" (Job 14:5 NIV).

The Bible also warns us to turn to
Christ immediately and not to wait:

- "Seek the LORD while he may be found; call on him while he is near" (Isaiah 55:6 NIV).

- "So you also must be ready, because the Son of Man will come at an hour when you do not expect him" (Matthew 24:44 NIV).

- "And I will say to my soul, 'Soul, you have many goods laid up for many years; take your ease; eat, drink, *and* be merry.' But God said to him, 'Fool! This night your soul will be required of you; then whose will those things be which you have provided?'" (Luke 12:19–20 NKJV).

- "And now why are you waiting? Arise and be baptized, and wash away your sins, calling on the name of the Lord" (Acts 22:16 NKJV).

- "For God says, 'At just the right time, I heard you. On the day of salvation, I helped you.' Indeed, the 'right time' is now. Today is the day of salvation" (2 Corinthians 6:2 NLT).

- "That is why the Holy Spirit says, 'Today when you hear his voice, don't harden your hearts as Israel did when they rebelled, when they tested me in the wilderness'" (Hebrews 3:7–8 NLT).

Nowhere in the Bible can we find any encouragement to consider turning to the Savior *someday*. The Bible tells us to respond to the message of salvation *today*.

Q—Several months ago, a dear friend of mine was diagnosed with a terminal disease. He's literally days away from death, and he desperately wants to know if it is too late for him to turn to Christ.

A—Absolutely not! God's invitation to trust in Jesus for salvation is extended to anyone who is alive and who desires to spend eternity in heaven with God. The Bible doesn't require that a person be "saved" for a certain period of time in order to go to heaven after death.

Probably the best biblical example of a last-minute—or "deathbed"—conversion is found in Luke 23:39–43, which gives the account of a criminal who hangs dying on a cross next to Jesus. Only minutes before, this man had joined with the rest of the crowd at the scene of Jesus' crucifixion in mocking and insulting Him (see Matthew 27:44). But just minutes before he passed away into eternity, the criminal turned to Jesus and pleaded, "Jesus, remember me when you come into your kingdom" (Luke 23:42 NIV).

This was a true act of repentance. This criminal, who moments before had admitted that he deserved the punishment he was receiving for his crimes (vs. 41), reached out to Jesus and acknowledged that he needed the Savior. Jesus, seeing the desire in this man's heart to inherit the kingdom of God, turned and said to him, "Truly I tell you, today you will be with me in paradise" (vs. 43 NIV).

> As long as we draw breath, God's invitation stands.

As long as we draw breath, God's open invitation to come to the Savior for forgiveness and salvation stands.

Q—The Bible says that "God is love"—so how can a God who calls Himself love send anyone to hell for eternity?

A—A lot of Christians aren't comfortable talking about eternal punishment for unforgiven sinners, and they have a difficult time reconciling a loving God with eternity in hell. But the Bible is very clear that those whose sins are not covered through the sacrificial death of Jesus Christ face eternal punishment.

The New Testament has a lot to say

about eternal punishment for sinners. In fact, Jesus said these things about the reality of an eternal hell:

- "You have heard that our ancestors were told, 'You must not murder. If you commit murder, you are subject to judgment.' But I say, if you are even angry with someone, you are subject to judgment! If you call someone an idiot, you are in danger of being brought before the court. And if you curse someone, you are in danger of the fires of hell" (Matthew 5:21–22 NLT).

- "Don't be afraid of those who want to kill your body; they cannot touch your soul. Fear only God, who can destroy both soul and body in hell" (Matthew 10:28 NLT).

- "If your hand or your foot causes you to stumble, cut it off and throw it away. It is better for you to enter life maimed or crippled than to have two hands or two feet and be thrown into eternal fire. And if your eye causes you to stumble, gouge it out and throw it away. It is better for you to enter life with one eye than to have two eyes and be thrown into the fire of hell" (Matthew 18:8–9 NIV).

- "They [the unrighteous] will go away to eternal punishment, but the righteous will go to eternal life" (Matthew 25:46 NIV).

But Jesus wasn't the only New Testament figure who had things to say about hell. You can also find references to eternal punishment in the following passages: 2 Thessalonians 1:5–10; Jude 7, 13; Revelation 14:9–11, 20:10, 14–15.

If you're wondering how a loving God could send anyone to hell for eternity—or if you know someone who wonders the same thing—then you need to focus on what the Bible says about God's desire for people to know the Savior.

You can start with the apostle Peter's words in his second epistle: "The Lord isn't really being slow about his promise, as some people think. No, he is being patient for your sake. He does not want anyone to be destroyed, but wants everyone to repent" (2 Peter 3:9 NLT).

"The Lord is being patient for your sake."

Paul echoed Peter's words when he wrote, "I urge, then, first of all, that petitions, prayers, intercession and thanksgiving be made for all people—for kings and all those in authority, that we may live peaceful and quiet lives in all godliness and holiness. This is good, and pleases God our Savior, who wants all people to be saved and to come to a knowledge of the truth" (1 Timothy 2:1–4 NIV).

If you know someone you know needs the Savior but who has a hard time believing that a loving God would ever punish them for all eternity, it can helpful to point

them toward what the Bible says about
His loving provision of forgiveness and
salvation.

Here are some examples:

- "The next day John saw Jesus
  coming toward him and said,
  'Look! The Lamb of God who
  takes away the sin of the world!'"
  (John 1:29 NLT).

- "For God so loved the world, that
  He gave His only begotten Son,
  that whoever believes in Him shall
  not perish, but have eternal life"
  (John 3:16 NASB).

- "Very rarely will anyone die for
  a righteous person, though for a
  good person someone might possibly dare to die. But God demonstrates his own love for us in this:
  While we were still sinners, Christ
  died for us" (Romans 5:7–8 NIV).

- "That is why we labor and strive, because we have put our hope in the living God, who is the Savior of all people, and especially of those who believe" (1 Timothy 4:10 NIV).

- "But we see Jesus, who was made a little lower than the angels for the suffering of death, crowned with glory and honour; that he by the grace of God should taste death for every man" (Hebrews 2:9 KJV).

- "Christ also suffered once for sins, the just for the unjust, that He might bring us to God, being put to death in the flesh but made alive by the Spirit" (1 Peter 3:18 NKJV).

- "He is the atoning sacrifice for our sins, and not only for ours but also for the sins of the whole world" (1 John 2:2 NIV).

CONCLUSION

Ask people the question in the title of this book—*Why Do We Need a Savior?*—and chances are you'll get a number of different answers. Some may even tell you the question is moot, because humanity doesn't need a savior at all.

But the answer to that question doesn't come from human wisdom or experience. It comes from the heart of God through the Word of God. And God's Word, the Bible, says we most definitely need a savior.

As we conclude, let's revisit several points from this book's introduction. Regarding our need for a savior, the Bible teaches that:

- All humans since Adam and Eve sin by what they do and what they don't do, and that sin separates them from a holy God.

- We all deserve eternal punishment for our sin.

- There is nothing any of us can do on our own to escape God's judgment and earn a place in His eternal kingdom.

- In His loving compassion for people, and because He knew we needed a Savior, God has provided a door to His kingdom of heaven, in the person of Jesus Christ, who came to earth to live a sinless life, then die a sacrificial death for the sins of all humankind.

- God's offer of salvation is open to *all* people, no matter how badly they've messed up.
- We can access God's offer of salvation only through faith in Jesus Christ.

Having read this book, you know the truth—God's truth. The big question now is this: What will you do with that truth?

500 Questions & Answers from the Bible

For inquisitive readers of any age— adults and students alike—here's a book to shed light on the Bible's great questions. Where did the scripture come from? What is God really like? What do some of those confusing Bible passages really mean? More than 400 questions are answered in user-friendly language, based on sound Christian doctrine. Arranged in canonical order, *500 Questions & Answers from the Bible* is an excellent resource for regular Bible study. Its open design presents a wealth of information in an appealing, accessible format—and it's fully illustrated in col-or!

6" x 9" / 256 pages / Paperback

eHARLEQUIN.com

For **FREE online reading,** visit
www.eHarlequin.com now and enjoy:

Online Reads
Read **Daily** and **Weekly** chapters from
our Internet-exclusive stories by your
favorite authors.

Red-Hot Reads
Turn up the heat with one of our more
sensual online stories!

Interactive Novels
Cast your vote to help decide how these
stories unfold...then stay tuned!

Quick Reads
For shorter romantic reads, try our
collection of Poems, Toasts, & More!

Online Read Library
Miss one of our online reads?
Come here to catch up!

Reading Groups
Discuss, share and rave with other
community members!

For great reading online,
visit www.eHarlequin.com today!

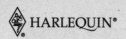

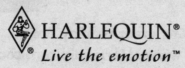

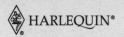

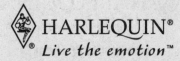

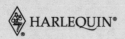
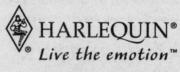